Uzbek Modern Storytelling

By:
Barno Eshmurzayeva

© Taemeer Publications LLC
Uzbek Modern Storytelling
by: Barno Eshmurzayeva
Edition: August '2023
Publisher:
Taemeer Publications LLC (Michigan, USA / Hyderabad, India)

ISBN 978-93-5872-133-1

© Taemeer Publications

Book   : *Uzbek Modern Storytelling*
Author   : Barno Eshmurzayeva
Publisher   : Taemeer Publications
Year   : '2023
Pages   : 42
Title Design : *Taemeer Web Design*

Table of Content

1	Image of human spirituality and psychology in the works of Abduqayum Yoldashev and Zulfiya Kurolboy's daughter	5
2	Image of human psyche in modern Uzbek storytelling	10
3	The interpretation of women's spirit in the story "ancient song" by Zulfiya Kurolboy's daughter	15
4	The principles of realism in prose of Zulfiya Kurolboy's daughter	18
5	Image of women in modern Uzbek stories	21
6	Tragedy in the stories of Zulfiya Kurolboy's daughter	27
7	Zulfiyakhanim is the embodiment of a true eastern woman	31
8	A new approach to the issue of women and girls in the new Uzbekistan	36

Eshmurzayeva Barno is the student of the Faculty of Uzbek Language and Literature of JDPU named after A. Qadiri. She is the daughter of Barno Osman.

IMAGE OF HUMAN SPIRITUALITY AND PSYCHOLOGY IN THE WORKS OF ABDUQAYUM YOLDASHEV AND ZULFIYA KUROLBOY'S DAUGHTER

Annotation:
In this article, the works of Abduqayum Yoldashev and Zulfiya Kurolboy's daughter talk about the illumination of human feelings, which are becoming a serious problem for the people of the present time.

Keywords:
literature, human feelings, image, language of artistic work, value, era, artistic work.

"If literature lives, the nation lives." These thoughts expressed by our great modern writer Cholpon, who deeply understood the fate of the nation in the last century, are increasingly being expressed. After all, literature is a means of educating the nation. People who know how to direct this tool correctly are talented and enthusiastic writers. It is not an exaggeration to say that in the era of Ahli Kalam, in the post-independence period, there is a real period of literature in our country. Let's take a look at the works of Abduqayum Yoldoshev and Zulfia Kurolboy, among our writers who skillfully reflect the human spirit and the image of the era through their works.

In Abduqayum Yoldoshev's stories, concepts such as human feelings, disappearing values, and sincerity, which are becoming urgent problems for the people of the present day, find their real expression. In the writer's work "Lies and Truth", the education of today's youth and the son's attitude towards his parents are reflected in the course of events. The story begins with the sentence "Raimberdi from Uzbekovul, the youngest son of a lame man, Gazikul, stayed in the city after graduation." And under the influence of this, the reader enters the atmosphere of the work, where nationalism is blowing. The names "Uzbekovullik" and "Rayimberdi Cholak" give an Uzbek spirit. In the play, the "goat seen by the city" - Ghazikul's lies and shamelessness of his parents, bowed down in front of the people, is depicted pitifully during the course of events. It creates mutual conflict between brothers. In Neksiya, which he won from the lottery, Gozikul promises to take his parents to visit Bukhara on Friday, but after several Fridays, there is no sign of him. "Old man Rayimberdi waited for one Friday, two Fridays, three Fridays... Every morning the father gets dressed without knowing. If Mabodo Ghaziboy arrives at "Neksiya", he is afraid to be in a hurry." Every time his son comes to ask for money, the father always believes his son's words, because in Uzbeks, parents do not want their children to suffer in any situation. In the process of giving money to his son, the writer equates money to a sheep as a means of image based on the Uzbek environment. "Each of you will give one sheep." Adib skillfully uses expressions and vernacular language to explain the events of the work: "My work is divided into five", "Khorozkand is like a young boy who was promised", why are you stretching like a bitter intestine", "he was saving from his pension for "death", "oh my father" it's worth talking about." These tools increase the expressiveness and color in the work. It helps the language of the work of art. The facelessness of the child is the cause of the decline of parents.

Adib refers the conclusion to the reader himself. The children took him to the hospital. The father died in pain in the district hospital... Until the last second, tears did not escape from the father's eyes, which were becoming more and more dim..." ["Lies and Truths" anthology of stories of the 20th century].

Through the work, the writer draws attention to the issue of youth education, which is an urgent problem today. In the acclaimed story "Poincaré", the problems of the time, the unhealthiness of the environment are considered as human degradation. In the first interpretations of the work, the variety of ideas and the unique aspects of performance skills are observed. "... "Poincaré" takes a worthy place due to its modernity, unique storytelling style, relevance of the artistic problem and, most importantly, the antiquity, accuracy, and historical-scientific basis of the puzzle at the center of the work. But despite having so many qualities, this work has nothing to do with postmodernism. Perhaps this is the novelty and originality of the work." [Uzok Dzhorakulov. "Khos kalam hosiyati" Tashkent. 2013.]

This story draws our attention to our pain points and flaws in our society. The rapid passing of life suggests that precious time is flowing in the ocean of marital ups and downs, that life is not only about needs. The fate of the main character of the play begins to swim according to the current of the environment from the time he was "beshikkerti" at the age of 5, he gets away from his desire due to his "interested teacher", his wife's whims and fancies throw him far away from his goal. These are the reasons why a person becomes ineffective. "I am also human. Live a little for myself, work a little for my youthful dreams." ["Poincaré". "Akademnashr" publishing house, Tashkent. 2014.]

The number of our "Heroes" whose dreams are shattered due to the influence of time and environment continues to increase. And we should not let it happen anymore. After all, society is the basis of the state. The work ends with the following sentences of our hero: "My God, take me back 30 years... take me back, my God..." God created man higher than the angels. Therefore, every person has the right to spend his life meaningfully. Our hero is partly to blame for this fate. If he had taken a bolder step towards his goal, it could have been completely different. In this respect, we see the lack of determination in the human spirit, and we try not to repeat these things in our lives. In his interviews, the writer expresses his thoughts about humanity and the environment: "There is light, there is shadow. Life is not just black and white, it is as colorful as a rainbow. Therefore, it is certain that everyone cannot be brought up in the same mold". [Abdurazzok Obro'yev. "The Pomegranate of Salmogi Kuva". November 29, 2021.]

In Zulfiya Kurolboy's story "Summerless Year", unlike the hero of "Poincaré", the character of Mother is depicted as a strong, determined character who cannot be swayed by the opinions and words of the people around her.

A mother sets before herself only the happiness and health of her son and acts boldly. It is true that both the heroes of these two works are in a helpless and depressed situation, but there is a difference in their relationship to the society and how strongly they act in relation to their situation. The hero of Adiba's story "Tafakkur", like the hero of the story "Poincaré", is a victim of bitter fate due to his father's ego due to his talent and dreams. Both works could have a positive ending, if they were not tormented by material things, if they were supported by the people around them.

In this regard, the stories of Zulfia Kurolboy's daughter also express the human spirit and its steps towards its dreams. In Adiba's story "Pictures of Stopped Time" it is reflected that a person should not stop moving, should grow his thinking as much as possible and raise his intelligence and spirituality. In this work, TIME, PERIOD, HUMAN SPIRITUALITY, SPIRITUALITY are described as the main concepts. Zulfia Kurolboy's daughter expresses these concepts in her "artistic language": a language close to the character and lifestyle of the people. Abduqayum Yoldoshev's "artistic skill" is reflected in the "finding plot" of current topics. After all, the freedom of creativity is not about "what to write", but also about "how to write". The works of Zulfiya Kurolboy's daughter hardly have an ending. This is also a unique style.

In general, every writer, whether he works in prose or poetry, creates a work of art in relation to society, environment, and human experience. Because literature studies a person not separately, but in an integral relationship with society and nature. It serves to educate people spiritually. After all, the main task of literature is to educate people in the spirit of hatred for evil and love for goodness.

References:

1. Abdurazzak Obroyev. "Pomegranate of Salmogi Kuva". November 29, 2021.
2. Long Dzhorakulov. "Khos kalam hosiyati" Tashkent. 2013.
3. "Poincare". "Akademnashr" publishing house, Tashkent. 2014.
4. "Lies and Truth" anthology of stories of the 20th century

Image of human psyche in modern Uzbek storytelling

ANNOTATION:
In modern storytelling, we can see that writers have deviated from the rules of some genres. The stories are written in a somewhat free manner, so that the writer writes what he wants. This requires that the theory of literature should be reviewed from another point of view. The relevance of this article is determined by the need to study genre changes occurring in modern stories.

Keywords:
literature, story, genre, composition, conflict, personality.

Enter

The story genre differs from other genres in terms of its size, composition, style, language and other artistic aspects. Although small in size, the narrative genre has its own challenges. We have great writers who skillfully put big topics into small stories. A. Qahhor, S. Ahmad, G'. Ghulam, etc., especially in the stories of A. Qahhor, we can feel the whole society and atmosphere in one sentence. It also describes the composition in a couple of sentences. In modern storytelling, the scope of the topic has changed.

"Today, the creator of our country, as in the ancient literature of the East, has focused his attention on the supreme human being, his soul. And the complex inner processes are not only written down by means of narration (there is such a way, it happens, and it is very natural), but at the same time, relying on universal and universal criteria, they put it down on paper and turn it into art by means of Majoz.[i] In fact, in modern Uzbek storytelling, the author focuses on revealing the inner psyche of a person, which is important at a time when problems related to human consciousness and psychology are increasing all over the world. For example, this is reflected in the stories created by our writers such as A. Yoldoshev, S. Vafo, Zulfiya Kurolboy qizi, N. Eshonqul, T. Mahmudov, H. Dostmuhammad, E. Azam, O. Otakhanov. The concept of human individuality is highlighted in stories in one way or another. For example, in the stories of Zulfiya Kurolboy's daughter, the psyche of each character is revealed in a different way.

"... we dream of achieving the status of good writers, we feathered penmen one day asked: What should be done to become a good student? The teacher answered: enter the reading with concentration and reflection, try to improve the most subtle aspects of the work in your hand.[ii]

Research method and methodology.

In each story of Zulfia Kurolboy's daughter, unique characters, special plots, concepts of goodness and evil in society are expressed. Adiba conveys the idea, the conclusion to the reader. Unknowingly, the reader falls into the role of the hero of the century and involuntarily feels his joys, pains and sorrows. He eagerly waits for the development, resolution, and conclusion of the events in the play.

In Adiba's stories "Summerless Year", as well as "Why does the sun rise?", "Queen of Unhappiness", the complicated situation in which the characters fell, the changes in their fate, nature, and psyche at that time are an expression of the skill of kindness and noble feelings. Whirlwind of hardships", it is completely different from the novels "Prisoner of Armon"1.

Discussion and results

The author's stories such as "Ayol", "Bride", "Shadow", "Ancient Song", "Uncle Khaliq" attract the reader with their strong emotions. Especially the story "Yozsiz yil" reflects pure Uzbek views on life. Aunt Buvgul, the main character in the play, embodies the image of a kind, compassionate mother who is ready to give everything for her child's only happiness. "Buvgul aunt was deeply shaken when a little boy who was walking like the wind was suddenly paralyzed and crippled due to a car accident. "What happens now? "Will my child live alone for the rest of his life?", of course, burned his wife, but when his son's life was on the line like a fly, these thoughts rose from his imagination and became completely insignificant"2 . Aunt Buvgul's son, Sabir, looks like a slob from the outside. his internal organs were badly crushed, one kidney had failed. He was forbidden by doctors to do heavy work. He felt a little better only on hot summer days. As Sabir grew up, he became more capricious and nervous. Aunt Buvgul took care of her son and tried to fulfill all his wishes. When the doctors said that Sabir had only two years left to live, aunt Buvgul seemed to lose herself. The life of the mother and child was spent in hospital after hospital, and her eldest son Mamatkul was responsible for her livelihood. He wanted to be a support to his mother and tried to do so. But soon, Mamatqul slapped his brother because Sabir had a quarrel with his fiancee due to his capriciousness. Aunt Buvgul was forced to move Mamatqul with her family to a house that was not yet completed. As time passed, Sabir grew up, the two years that the doctors said had passed. Meanwhile, a new page began to open in Sabir's life, that is, he fell in love. He confided in his mother about this and told his lover Marvarid that he was going to marry her. This news was both happy and sad for Aunt Buvgul. He did not want to break his son's heart even though he knew that he would be rejected when he went to the wedding. "... I know well that I have no right to take away someone's daughter, even if no one bothers me, but you can't stand it when your child is staring at you..."3. Despite Mamatqul's objections, Majid's brother calling him a madman, and the whole village's talk, he went to court for his child several times. The girl's wedding took place and Sabir became addicted to alcohol. The fact that her child's health was getting worse and closer to death was exhausting the mother more and more. He had to stand without medicine. "I wish I could die before I see these days," thought Aunt Buvgul. But soon he repented and took back what he had said. - If you die, who will take care of your child, you fool! If you say that your child should not be humiliated, ask God for your life!"4. - If you die, who will take care of the child, idiot! If you say that your child should not be humiliated, ask God for your life!"4. - If you die, who will take care of the child, idiot! If you say that your child should not be humiliated, ask God for your life!"4.

Soon the news spread that Pearl had returned from Earth. Sabir felt as if he had lost his life again. His mother could not say no to his desire to go to courtship. But Majid returned quietly after hearing bitter words from his brother's doorstep. Marvarid was sent away in marriage to a distant mountain place. The mother burned and cried with her child.

Mamatkul sometimes got angry with her mother because she was alone with Sabir: "No one has anything to do with me..." she began to cry shaking her shoulders. "No one has anything to do with me..."5. Even though these words were hard, Aunt Buvgul swallowed everything inside, because she is a mother... She could not say "no" to her child even if the whole world was against her, because she is a mother...

This year, winter came hard. Sabir was bedridden. Aunt Buvgul was a butterfly in the eyes of her child with her sickly look. He was hoping that the winter would end earlier, and that Sabir's condition would improve with the arrival of spring and the start of hot summer days. Summer has come. Sabir passed away on the fifteenth day of June. "The mother, who was leaning against the pillar of the porch, muttering, repeated one word: - I'm bad, you're good, my child... and then, suddenly, staring at the sky, which was spewing fire, she was whispering like a merchant: - because you created a person for fun, and you couldn't feed him then did you think of death?.. Since you have plenty of fire, why didn't you give it in time?!."6

Summary

In all of Adiba's works, the human personality is put in the first place. In the stories, the experiences of the heroes, their rebellion against fate, involuntarily prompts a person to think. Adiba throws the reader into the flow of life, but this flow is mixed with the author's aesthetic idea, matlab. As a result, the reader perceives life "without the intervention of the author". It is the same in the novels of Zulfia Kurolboy's daughter "Arman Asira" and "Mashqatlar Girdobi". Adiba, especially, describes the image of women with strong willed qualities. Their internal conflict is skillfully revealed during the plot. The analyzes were conducted on the basis of the works of Zulfia Kurolboy's daughter "O, Hayot", "Whirlpool of Difficulties", "Captive of Armon", "Summerless Year", "Thafakkur", "Shadow", "Ikki Manzil".

[1] Umarali Normatov - from the article "Benazir Ziya in the heart".

[2] Zulfia Kurolboy's daughter. "The year without summer". Tashkent: Uzbekistan.

[3] Zulfia Kurolboy's daughter. "The year without summer". Tashkent: Uzbekistan.

[4] Zulfia Kurolboy's daughter. "The year without summer". Tashkent: Uzbekistan.

[5] Zulfia Kurolboy's daughter. "The year without summer". Tashkent: Uzbekistan.

[6] Zulfia Kurolboy's daughter. "The year without summer". Tashkent: Uzbekistan.

THE INTERPRETATION OF WOMEN'S SPIRIT IN THE STORY "ANCIENT SONG" BY ZULFIYA KUROLBOY'S DAUGHTER

Abstract:
In this scientific article, the inner experiences and psyche of Shahsanam, the main character in the story "Ancient Song" by our writer Zulfia Kurolboy, who became famous for her stories in today's Uzbek short story writing and skillfully embodied female characters in her stories, are analyzed.
Keywords:
Love, suffering, loneliness, psyche, desire.

The works written on the image of a woman and her spirit are among the works that are timeless and distinguished by their vitality in all times and places. The beautiful aspects of the image of a woman are revealed in Uzbek literature in the works of Miss Zulfia Kurolboy, Salamatkhan Vafoeva, Jamila Ergasheva and a number of other writers. In particular, we can see beautiful examples of a woman's image in almost all the stories of Zulfiya Kurolboy's daughter. Adiba, focusing on the image of a woman, creates her dreams, aspirations, goals, and psyche in a very impressive way. The story unfolds before the eyes of the reader. The story "Ancient Song" also depicts female characters, and the spirit of the main character of the story, Shahsanam, greatly affects the reader and brings him pity. The main character of the story, Shahsanam, gets married as a second wife to Eshan, who treated her for her illness. The reason for this is not clear to anyone. Not long after that, Eshon died, and Shahsanam was left alone in the courtyard. Of course, this affects his mental health and well-being. "It's all... because I'm tight..." Shahsanam said brokenly. His face was saffron, his eyes were old, and his thin body was extremely weak. Shahsanam was fading day by day. The reason for her depression was that, on the one hand, she was alone, and on the other hand, her childhood love turned into a dream. Even so, the woman could not lose her heart from her lover, living with him gave her happiness and encouraged her to live life. She also had the right to be happy as a woman. Sultan Murad, who encouraged the lonely Shahsanam, gradually brought her back to life. "Every change in his state of mind did not go unnoticed by the young man: "Today he spoke for more than half an hour, he spoke calmly and without anger. Even his laughter began to ring out...". Unfortunately, this woman's happiness and joy will not last long. "Shohsanam woke up in the middle of the night from a thunderclap, and suffered an unbearably painful heart attack for twenty minutes, and ... handed over his deposit."

If the reader is surprised by the thunder that struck the earth like a light despite the temperature being forty degrees, then he will feel sorry for the young man who left this world early because of that thunder. This event fills the reader with deep thoughts.

Nevertheless, whether these two lovers do not want to leave each other, or because this separation affected Sultanmurad very much, even after Shahsanam's death, he came to Sultanmurad's side: "The young man who passed by the window suddenly stopped 'khtadi. - You ?! - Yes, I... - After all, you... - I couldn't go!" At this point, the writer Shahsanam explains why she does not want to leave this world, even though her soul has left her body, but she cannot leave this world: "The world is so beautiful! It's enough to live and breathe... How wonderful is the rustling of leaves in the moonlight... But... I love this world because of your presence. Because of you!" When Sultan Murad is about to commit suicide, Shahsanam appears in his eyes and tries to dissuade him by crying out to take him from this world. In this place, the writer talks about the death of Shahsanam, her helplessness, how she will suffer in the afterlife if she lives with Sultan Murad in this world, and if she leaves this world early and her late husband follows her, she will find happiness in the next world. Although Sultan Murad did not leave this world, his mind had completely left. That love made Sultanmurad mad and Shahsanam unhappy.

The work mainly depicts two female characters, one of them is Shahsanam, and the second female character is her relative and Sultan Murad's wife. The writer has described them in his own way. If Sultan Murad's wife is depicted as being interested in the lives of others and paying less attention to her husband, instead of paying attention to her husband and family, the image of Shahsanam is embodied as a kind and gentle woman to her beloved. It is no exaggeration to say that the creation of such contrasting female characters in the story ensured its effectiveness and vitality.

Zulfia Kurolboy was able to show the most delicate and intimate aspects of a woman's spiritual world through her stories. His stories are distinguished by their harmony with life events, without any exaggeration, and we would not be mistaken if we say that the writer held a mirror to life through his stories. At this point, we can see that the following thoughts of Umarali Normatov are appropriate: "After Sister Saida, we have before our eyes a talented writer who exudes an elegant Uzbek sophistication and at the same time a brave courage and a sense of justice in her works. I consider it a happy event for our national prose. Indeed, Zulfia Kurolboy's daughter was able to show her talent in Uzbek literature and won a place in the hearts of readers.

References:

1. Zulfiya Kurolboy's daughter "Woman". -T. Gafur Ghulam Publishing House, 2005
2. Umarov H. "Fundamentals of artistic creativity". Uzbekistan-Tashkent. 2001
3. Kayumov L. "Contemporaries". Literary and art publishing house named after Gafur Ghulam - Tashkent, 1985
4. Normatov U. "Magic of creativity". - Tashkent. East. 2007

THE PRINCIPLES OF REALISM IN PROSE OF ZULFIYA KUROLBOY'S DAUGHTER

Annotation:
Zulfia Kurolboy's stories and novels stand out among the works created in Uzbek literature due to their interestingness, impressiveness, realistic portrayal of human characters, and bold handling of complex life problems. The fact that the works of Z. Kurolboy's daughter have risen to the level of a serious phenomenon in literature determines the relevance of this article.

Keywords:
literature, Zulfiya, prose, realism, ideology.

For a long time, literary studies have adapted to examine the work of art mainly from the social point of view, but now, leaving the existing scientific patterns, it tries to approach it as a spiritual-emotional magical phenomenon based on aesthetic requirements.

In the current period of social renewal, great changes and development are taking place in the human personality, as a result of which the knowledge of the spiritual and spiritual world of students is becoming complex, and spiritual awakening and ideological renewal are felt in their minds . This process requires looking for ways to increase the impact of presenting examples of fiction to students. Although a wide range of scientific studies have been published in Uzbek literary studies on the analysis of works of art, until now there are still few cases of examining and presenting the work to the reader in terms of topical relevance and social significance. In the study of a work of art, the artistic text itself is the first place, and the age, party affiliation, gender, and experience of any creator are completely unimportant.

Zulfia Kurolboy's stories and novels stand out among the works created in Uzbek literature for their interestingness, impressiveness, convincing embodiment of the reality of life and human characters, and for boldly raising the complex problems of life. In the works of the author, the characters, events, and endings that the reader is used to do not meet. These works have become an artistic phenomenon that cannot be ignored in Uzbek literature, and have gained their readers. Researching its specific features, determining its internal mechanism, the factors that ensure its artistry will allow a full understanding of current literature. Due to this necessity, this topic was tackled.

The purpose of the study. Based on the research and analysis of the works of Zulfiya Kurolboy's daughter, it is necessary to determine the specific aspects of the Uzbek literature of the independence period and the unique features of the creative prose works.

Research tasks:
- to determine the theoretical principles of the story and the direction of the image, the stages of development;
- monitoring and analyzing the news about the expression of national and universal values in literary stories;
- To determine the factors that ensure the originality of Zulfiya Kurolboy's work.

Research source. "Captive of Armenia" written by Zulfiya Kurolboy

The novels "Whirlpool of Troubles", "Ayol", "Hilola", "Oh, Life!", "Tafkkur", "Ikki Manzil", "Shadow" and similar stories were examined as a source of research.

The level of study of the problem. Although the talented writer Zulfia Kurolboy enriches the treasure of our spirituality with a series of works that have raised the level of a serious phenomenon in literature, until today there are no studies in literary studies that analyze her work in detail. Until now, articles by literary scholars such as Umarali Normatov, Kazoqboy Yoldashev, Nusratilla Jumakhoja, Khurshid Dostmuhammad have been published on the author's works. Nilufar Heydarova compared the novel "Arman Asirasi" with the novel "Makon Istab" written by Jenny Erpenbek, Israilova In the works of Caodat Adiba, for example, there are graduate theses that examined the place of evolutions in the spirituality of the nation in the current narrative. In particular, Nilufar

Haydarova believes that there is a connection between the main character of the novel "Makon istab" by the German writer Jenny Erpenbeck and Hulkar Armon, the hero of the novel "Armon Asira" by Zulfia Kurolboy. Both novels are based on people's desire to reach their native place, to create their own place.

Summary

By gradually researching the creative maturity of Zulfia Kurolboy's daughter from the time she entered the world of artistic creation until today, an attempt was made to show the reasons for the unique characteristics, achievements and shortcomings of the writer's prose works. In particular, many main features of the young writer's prose have been identified in the examples of the author's novels "Prisoner of Armon", "Whirlpool of Troubles" and several stories. Such characteristics include the author's deep artistic research of the female heart and character and the desire to express the truth about them, the plot is interesting and often unconventional, the problems of life are courageously covered, and noble social ideals are confirmed.

References:

1. Literary types and genres. 3 volumes. Volume 1. Under the editorship of Academician B. Nazarov. - T., 1991.

2. Henry Barbus. Zolya v 1932. V knige "Nazwvat vern,i svoimi imenami". - M.: 1986, S. 76.

3. Aristotle. Poetics. - T.: "Literature and Art", 1980.

4. Akhmedova. M. Julio Cortázar: a scene from the spiritual life of the 20th century. World literature. 2009, October.

5. Boboev T. "Basics of Literary Studies" Tashkent. 2002, pp. 470-471.

IMAGE OF WOMEN IN MODERN UZBEK STORIES

Abstract:
In this article, the characteristic aspect of the image of Uzbek women is analyzed based on the stories of Zulfia Kurolboy, a bright representative of modern Uzbek literature. By creating the characters of various characters such as Nazokat, Aunt Buvgul, and Tamara in the stories "Ayol", "Yozziz Yil", "Victim of Loneliness", appropriate conclusions were drawn based on the analysis of the artist's skills.

Keywords:
image, character, prose, interpretation, analysis, word, artistry, realism, spirit, skill, creative skill.

Since the first years of independence, fundamental changes have taken place in the development of Uzbek literature, like all other fields. This was especially evident in prose. The originality of form and content, a new interpretation of the artist's style has appeared, which, of course, has the influence of advanced creative traditions characteristic of world literature. Most of these innovations in prose were reflected in the fast and concise narrative genre. In fact, regardless of the genre of prose, the main image in it is the image of a person.

"In order for a literary work to be a true example of a work, whether it belongs to realism, is written in the style of romanticism, or follows some other modernist style, it still needs a human being in its center, the reader receives certain information about the fate, nature, and life of a person, and also gets aesthetic pleasure from this work. let him be able to take it too." Therefore, in modern literature, comprehensive study and discovery of man does not lose its constant relevance. Literature is rich and beautiful not only in terms of style, form and interpretation, but also in the variety of characters created in artistic works. Depicting characters who fight for life, strive for goodness, have patience and intelligence is the educational and aesthetic task of fiction. Today, Zulfia Kurolboy is one of the female writers who has created such diverse characters and has a place in the field of literature. In the stories created by him, the image of a woman has a special place. In particular, the author skillfully created various characters such as Nazokat, Aunt Buvgul, and Tamara in the stories "Ayol", "Yozsiz yil", "Victim of Loneliness" by his pen, which once again shows the reader that the writer has a high taste and talent. will confess. Through these images, their spiritual experiences, the sufferings and thoughts of the owners of different destinies are attractively and realistically interpreted artistically. In each of the women in her stories, in addition to the feelings of originality, love, loyalty and loyalty, characteristics such as determination and will are also developed.

The image of Nazokat in the story "Woman" is a clear example of this. In addition to the patience and feelings of love characteristic of Uzbek women, oriental elegance and strength will be more clearly expressed in determining the character of the character. While tenderness is fighting with severe pain, sira does not give up on femininity. He does not abandon his grace and beauty, he knows that he will give up his life with this beauty, and no matter how much pain prevails, no matter how much he tries to pass his judgment on him, he will not be defeated by these difficulties, he prefers to fight valiantly, he will not despair even for a moment. After her death, a woman dreams of remaining in the memory of her family, children and husband as a kind mother, a beautiful wife. She is a tenacious woman who strives to live up to her name and is ready for anything. She feels that she has only a few days left in her life, she spends her few moments to find death while preserving her feminine femininity.

She does not want to be remembered by her husband and children as a woman whose face is pale, her eyes are sleepless and without light, and her body is overcome with swelling and pain. This can be observed in the following passage: "A nurse entered the ward. If my husband comes, please don't let him in - Nazokat told him. Why? "The doctor has appointed someone to be with you at night," said the nurse. Do not enter for a while, please. But he is worried... You will come up with an excuse! - said Nazokat and put money in the nurse's pocket. The nurse left hesitantly. Nazokat stared at the window. His sons appeared before his eyes. The woman bit her lip hard not to burst out. Through this dialogue, the writer convincingly wrote down the pain and suffering of the woman, which ensured the liveliness and aesthetic effect of the work. She does not want to show her husband her ugly and faded state after the swellings have taken over her whole body. She convinces the nurse not to let her husband in for money. She is depicted in a double struggle: pain occupying her body and efforts to preserve her beauty and femininity. Femininity is ready to endure all the pains of the world in order to die a beautiful death and keep her femininity forever. He expects only one thing from the doctors: that he will not die ugly, that he will bear all the pain, and expects salvation from them. He sewed everything on this road, even a gold ring: "Nazokat put the gold ring in the doctor's pocket. Take the water, please. Only to the end! The doctor did not answer again. He didn't even look at it. Even after the woman's hand went into his pocket, he did not look at her face. However, "Nurse!" he called, looking at the corridor. Beauty smiles. Then he took the upa-elik from under his pillow...".

The most impressive part of the story, which moves the reader and immediately makes him cry, the highest point of pain and suffering, is that the ghost of death, despite the fact that he is walking in the fire, is next to the upa- elik pillow and takes it. He manifests his will like a moth. We are once again convinced that the author of the high and vivid image of reality is a real talent, the sharpness of his pen, and the possession of high taste and quality. Another such story of Zulfia Kurolboy's daughter is "Yozsiz yil". Although the character of aunt Buvgul in the story is very different from Nazokat, they have some similarities. Aunt Buvgul is saddened to see the endless pain and suffering of her son, who lost his health and manhood due to a car accident, and despite being completely overwhelmed by grief, she is so patient that she forgets everything because of her son's one smile. - we can see the image of a real Uzbek woman who is patient, even forgets herself and gives everything for the happiness of her child.

The author tried to convey the images in the story to all the readers and he succeeded. A woman's mood, inner pain, is idealized in artistic colors to the extent that it shakes the heart. The writer expressed the picture of his whirlwind of thoughts in this way: "How much longer will this situation continue?" But from the moment he saw the happy face of his son, he forgot everything, what will happen tomorrow, now there is no one happy with my son, what more do I need." Yes, she is ready to do anything to get rid of her child's pain, and at the same time she is a munificent and munificent mother. She hates everyone who looks down on her child. He even hates winter, which causes his child's health to deteriorate. She is the epitome of a real Uzbek mother whose only reason to live is for her child. His image is enriched with artistic tools and turned into a beautiful landscape. It is clear from every action and speech that the writer has accomplished the task assigned to him in the truest sense. She created the image of a truly devoted mother.

In Adiba's story "Victim of Loneliness", a completely different world, a different life is written. The main character in it is a representative of another world. The story refers to the image of a lonely woman. It is clear from the title of the story that a woman trapped by loneliness is tragically described as passing through the world silently and without any sign. It is clearly explained that a woman is childless, unable to keep a child even though she is very old, and raising a child seems like an impossible task for her. It embodies the features of a woman who shied away from responsibility, lived only for herself, lived through youth and indolence without realizing the terrible and sad end of old age and loneliness. After losing her husband, she remains alone. In order to get rid of the loneliness and desolation that eats him, he goes to visit his loved ones, he cannot find satisfaction anywhere, he is not satisfied, and he returns to those useless things. Loneliness dries him up to such an extent that he even convinces himself that the rats have found him, he is happy, this situation seems very unusual when you think about it. He will die in loneliness from this useless and meaningless life. That night, a thief broke into his house and lost the things that he considered dear all his life, that he thought were more valuable than a child. At the end of the work, the woman becomes a victim of loneliness. this situation seems very unusual when you think about it. He will die in loneliness from this useless and meaningless life. That night, a thief broke into his house and lost the things that he considered dear all his life, that he thought were more valuable than a child. At the end of the work, the woman becomes a victim of loneliness. this situation seems very unusual when you think about it. He will die in loneliness from this useless and meaningless life. That night, a thief broke into his house and lost the things that he considered dear all his life, that he thought were more valuable than a child. At the end of the work, the woman becomes a victim of loneliness.

Summary

Generally speaking, three types of female characters are depicted in the above analyzed stories of Zulfiya Kurolboy's daughter. The writer has very clearly and convincingly expressed the human psyche, the fundamental twists and turns in his fate, and mental anguish. His sharp language and artistry combined to create beautiful works of art. In current literature, more attention is paid to the analysis of the human psyche than to the description of reality. It should be said that in the works of the writer, not social issues, but the image of a particular person, especially the image of a woman, and the description of his experiences and feelings are leading. In his works, the writer tries to satiate the artistic reality he created for the reader and make it understandable. For today's writers, realistic life is not the first priority. It is considered a means of ensuring artistic reality. The works of art are not about the details of interesting events, but about human experiences. In this regard, the image of a woman, the character of a woman requires constant study.

References:
1. The story of Zulfiya Kurolboy's daughter "Ayol". Ziya.uz. 2013.
2. The story of Zulfiya Kurolboy's daughter "The Summerless Year". "Youth" magazine. 2017.
3. The story of Zulfiya Kurolboy's daughter "Victim of Loneliness". Ziya.uz. 2013.

TRAGEDY IN THE STORIES OF ZULFIYA KUROLBOY'S DAUGHTER

Annotation:
Zulfiya Kurolboy's stories and novels stand out among the works created in Uzbek literature for their interestingness, impressiveness, convincing embodiment of the reality of life and human characters, as well as the bold handling of complex problems of life. The fact that Z. Kurolboy's daughter's works have risen to the level of a serious phenomenon in literature determines the relevance of this article.

Keywords:
literature, Zulfiya, prose, realism, ideology, spirituality, suffering, pain, illness, love.

Zulfiya Kurolboy's daughter (Zulfiya Yoldosheva) was born on September 15, 1966 in Jizzakh district of Jizzakh region. Jizzakh graduated from the Faculty of Uzbek Philology of the Pedagogical Institute. (1990). He published books such as "Life" (2003), "Angel of Evil" (2005). For a long time, literary studies have adapted to examine the work of art mainly from the social point of view, but now, leaving the existing scientific patterns, it is trying to approach it as a spiritual-emotional magical phenomenon based on aesthetic requirements.

During the current period of social renewal, great changes and development are taking place in the human personality, as a result of which the knowledge of the spiritual and spiritual world of students is becoming complex, and spiritual awakening and ideological renewal are felt in their minds . This process requires finding ways to increase the effectiveness of presenting examples of fiction to students. Although a wide range of scientific studies have been published in Uzbek literary studies on the analysis of artistic works, until now there are still few cases of examining and presenting the work to the reader in terms of topicality and social importance. In the study of a work of art, it is not always remembered that the artistic text itself is the first place, and the age, party affiliation, gender, and experience of any creator are completely unimportant. Now the tasks before literary studies have changed: to study the work based only on the text and to conclude according to the nature of the text. Uzbek literature of the period of independence is characterized by the fact that it violates the formed ideas about genres, and the created works do not correspond to theoretical laws and regulations.

After all, the freedom of creativity is not only about "what to write", but also about "how to write". The freedom to write as you wish allows you to conduct creative experiments. Prose is a significant part of today's literary process. Zulfia Kurolboy's daughter is one of the creators who made a great contribution to the development of modern Uzbek prose. Zulfia Kurolboy's stories and novels stand out among the works created in Uzbek literature for their interestingness, impressiveness, convincing embodiment of the reality of life and human characters, as well as boldly raising the complex problems of life. In the works of the author, the characters, events, and events that the reader is used to do not meet. These works have become an artistic phenomenon that cannot be ignored in Uzbek literature, and have gained their readers. Researching its specific features, determining its internal mechanism, and the factors that ensure its artistry allow a full understanding of current literature. Due to this necessity, this topic was tackled. The novels "Captive of Armon", "Whirlpool of Difficulties", "Ayol", "Hilola", "Oh, life!", "Tafakkur", "Ikki Manzil" written by Zulfiya Kurolboy's daughter. "Shadow" and similar stories were reviewed. "Hilola", "Oh, life!", "Tafakkur", "Ikki Manzil" written by Zulfiya Kurolboy's daughter. "Shadow" and similar stories were reviewed. "Hilola", "Oh, life!", "Tafakkur", "Ikki Manzil" written by Zulfiya Kurolboy's daughter. "Shadow" and similar stories were reviewed.

Although the talented writer Zulfiya Kurolboy enriched the treasury of our spirituality with a number of works that raised the level of a serious phenomenon in literature, until today there are no studies in literary studies that analyze her work in detail. Until now, articles by literary scholars such as

Umarali Normatov, Kazoqboy Yoldashev, Nusratilla Jumakhoja, Khurshid Dostmuhammad have been published on the author's works. Nilufar Haydarova compared the novel "Arman Asirasi" with the novel "Makon Istab" written by Jenny Erpenbek, Israilova In Saodat Adiba's works, for example, there are graduate theses that examined the place of evolutions in the spirituality of the nation in the current narrative . In particular, Nilufar Haydarova believes that there is a connection between the main character of the German writer Jenny Erpenbeck's novel Makon istab and Hulkar Armon, the hero of Zulfia Kurolboy's novel The Captive of Armon. According to Nilufar, the heroine of Jenny Erpenbek lost her place, her homeland as a result of a real war, while the heroine of Zulfia Kurolboy lost her place because of the eternal, invisible battle between her desire and livelihood.

Summary

In our opinion, this aspect ensures the vitality of Zulfia Kurolboy's works, awakens the reader, and in general determines the uniqueness of the literary work. By gradually researching the creative maturity of Zulfia Kurolboy's daughter from the time she entered the world of artistic creation until today, an attempt was made to show the reasons for the unique characteristics, achievements and shortcomings of the writer's prose works.

In particular, many main features of the young writer's prose have been identified in the examples of the author's novels "Armon Asira", "Whirlpool of Difficulties" and several stories. Such characteristics include the writer's deep artistic research of the female heart and character and the desire to express the truth about them, the interesting and often unconventional construction of the plot, the courageous coverage of life's problems, and the confirmation of noble social ideals. These characteristics Zulfia Kurolboy It was revealed through the analysis of his daughter's works "Ayol", "Hilola", "Oh, life!", "Tafakkur", "Ikki Manzil", "Shadow", "Whirlpool of hardships".

References:
1. Literary types and genres. 3 volumes. Volume 1. Under the editorship of Academician B. Nazarov. - T., 1991.
2. Aristotle. Poetics. - T.: "Literature and Art", 1980.
3. Akhmedova. M. Julio Cortázar: a scene from the spiritual life of the 20th century. World literature. 2009, October.
4. Boboev T. "Fundamentals of Literary Studies". Tashkent. 2002, pp. 470-471.

Zulfiyakhanim is the embodiment of a true Eastern woman

Abstract:
This article talks about the life and work of the famous poetess Zulfiya Israilova, her poems.

Keywords:
poem, creator, Motherland, Eastern woman, award, icon

Zulfiya is a real Uzbek woman, a smart girl, a courageous child of the country, a great and munificent poetess, a beloved and selfless mother... When it comes to Zulfiya Israilova, one hesitates to talk about which side of the poetess. Because the poetess is brilliant both as a person and as a creator.

Zulfiya was born in a simple family of a blacksmith, and from this simplicity, she created a glamorous and luxurious world for herself. Looking at his father's packing hands and the sparks coming out of the machines, he felt feelings of love, not hatred, towards work. From her mother, who has a wise heart, the knowledge of poetry began to grow in the poet's heart and thoughts. The poetess herself writes about it like this: "The love for words was awakened by a simple woman, my mother, who causes miracles, exposes the world, and leads humanity to the goals." "...Suddenly I began to notice that my thoughts were not expressed in simple words and phrases, but in a poetic way..."

Student years were a period of real creativity for the poetess, a period full of enthusiasm and enthusiasm. In 1932, when Zulfia was 17 years old, her first collection of poems called "Life Pages" was published. He wrote so many hot poems that he proved that he is a true descendant of Nadira, Uvaysi, Anbar Otin.

The person who brought Zulfiya to creative perfection and brought a world of love to her poems was her life partner Hamid Olimjon, the great poet of our nation. In 1935, two great talents got married. "I saw Hamid Olimjon for the first time that year," writes Zulfia. I'm not going to hide. Hamid Olimjon passed from my eyes to my heart from the first meeting. With my very young feelings, I sensed his broad heart and great talent."[1] The fire of happiness, which was extinguished in an instant, illuminated the life of the poetess for a lifetime. The death of H. Olimjon found Zulfia in the trials of life and separation, she was able to cope with her loss. Separation turned their love into a legend. Even though it is repeated over and over again, its value does not decrease even for a moment, and the hymns, which haunt every single woman and single mother, have been absorbed into our consciousness.

Flipping through the book of life

I did not regret the past life.

I smiled instead of a smile,

If I need to kiss, I kiss like crazy.

I don't care if I'm wearing silk or chit,

I don't care about the wealth of the heart,

The life that caressed me is like the sun,

Every lesson requires a new song.

I did not regret the past life,

I have never seen anyone like me in my life:

I loved

pampered

I left

I burned

I know what Izzat is.

Live at the same time!..

Zulfiyakhanim was not only a devoted child and a beloved wife, but also a passionate and strong-willed Mother. He took care of the children, who could be a soul to his life and a shield to his heart, like new sprouts in the world of pure and pure love, and brought them up as real people. Hulkar and Amon became the good news of life for the poetess, consolation of the soul, support of life:

I've lived a lifetime without you

Waiting for the return of eternal joys,

When I kneel at the head of your coffin,

The children took me by the hand.

Uzbek women have never been weak, the saying "a woman has forty souls" has not spread among our people in vain. Zulfia was one of those mothers, she was both a mother and a father for her children, she gave her forty lives to forty one worries. He never forgot his homeland, why he lived, and that he should help his people in a difficult situation as much as he could.

During the war, Zulfiya wrote his fiery poems and instilled the spirit of love and self-sacrifice into the hearts of the soldiers. He was able to help them. At that time, our whole nation would eat one raisin into forty pieces. Zulfia gave her share to her people through her heart-warming poems and calls to courage, and this was like water and air for our brave warriors to feel the fresh air of the country from the stuffy air of war at that time. was necessary.

How much confidence and hope it gives,

This language is for both the Motherland and me,

Out of my side like a rock

Lean on, he says, boldly on my wrist...²

Zulfia was not only a beloved country, but also a proud child for her country. His diltartar poems were heard all over the world, and his small homeland, Uzbekistan, was mentioned and described in large circles. Zulfiya was lucky enough to fulfill the duty that every child of the country should fulfill. They are the beloved servants of Allah... In the second half of the 50s, Zulfia actively participated in the movement of Asian and African writers, which took place under peace and international solidarity, and the poem "Mushoira" written during this period brought great fame to the poetess. Zulfia was awarded Jawaharlal Nehru and Nilufar international awards. Zulfia was a real Uzbek woman and child. The well-known Avar poet Rasul Hamzatov says: "When I learned about Zulfiya, When I met her personally at the writer's congress in Moscow, when I read her poems, I realized that she is a wonderful poet and a wonderful person, a wonderful Eastern woman who is a worthy representative of her motherland Uzbekistan. I will not hide, sometimes creative women are given concessions. But Zulfiya was not one of those people, she was a poet whose fate was connected with the fate of her people..." Russian writer Nikolay Tikhonov also emphasizes that she is a true woman of the East: "...She herself is like a new dawn to her friends. It is the Eastern woman who illuminates the³In fact, Zulfiya is recognized and applauded by the writers of the whole world. At the base of all of their words lies the idea that they recognized Zulfiya as a real Uzbek woman, a woman of the East, and that they understood it. With her virtues, Zulfia raised the meaning of the concept of Uzbek woman to the world.

What about us? Are we doing something worthy of the name Uzbek child? Can we be Zulfia's successor? Only a child who, like Zulfiyakhanim, has instilled the feeling of the Motherland in his blood and acquired sincerity, can become Musharraf in this name. Zulfiya Khanim's poems are always a melody that awakens slumbering souls...

Members, thank you for your support,

You are the sun, I am the light.

May your mornings laugh, medicine, hur,

That's my luck- I am Zulfia of Uzbek.

References:

1. Umirova A. Bakhtim shul - I am Zulfiya of Uzbek. People's word. 2020.
2. Israilova Z. My tunes are for you. Tashkent. 1965.
3. Karimov N. About sister Zulfiya. Uzbek history, literature and culture. 2013.

A NEW APPROACH TO THE ISSUE OF WOMEN AND GIRLS IN THE NEW UZBEKISTAN

Abstract:
This article talks about the reforms being carried out in Uzbekistan to protect and promote women's rights.
Keyword:
Women, gender equality, women scientists, women's rights, virtuous women.

A woman is a unique creature. The strong will, love and devotion given to him by Allah Almighty is the force that sustains and elevates the world and moves it. We can understand this by looking at the history of our nation. In the history of our country, among the great scientists and our world-loving ancestors, there were many virtuous women who gave birth to such people and inspired them to great deeds. In particular, we all know the bravery of To'maris, who has a place in the pages of distant history. The princess of the Massaget tribe managed to defeat the Persian Achaemenid king Cyrus II on the battlefield in 529 BC. During the time of Nadira, wife of Khan Umarkhan of Kokand, a representative of Uzbek classical literature, poets such as Uvaisi grew up, and a large literary environment was created in Kokand.

The great thinker Alisher Navoi in his book "Majolis un-nafois" gives information about some women artists who lived in that period. Although their names are not mentioned in the tazkira as individual authors, the scholar's notes about them are extremely important for literary studies. Alisher Navoi in the section dedicated to the poet Shaykhzada Ansari of the Tazkira gives information such as "I'm very good looking, and his parents are also known as Bedili", and in the section about Maulana Sulaimani: About the poem considered to be Sulaymani's. And I am a famous lunatic, this abyot belongs to Mehr, the wife of Maulana Sulaimani.*[2. 167]*,he writes.

In the book "Women Rulers in Islamic States" by the Turkish scientist, Ankara dorilfununi professor Bahria Uchak, the heroism of Tomaris, the princess of the Massagets who fought against the Iranian king Cyrus, is mentioned.

In the fight against the Arab invaders, Tugshada, the mother of the Sogdian prince Tugshad, who was one of the defenders of Turonzamin, showed bravery. He controlled the roads to the cities of Samarkand, Bukhara, and Amul, and defended his capital Poykent from the forces of Said ibn Usman Hajjaj and Qutayba.

"In the period of Jahiliyyah, women who had no rights and were considered the personal property of men, gained wide rights and opportunities when the Qur'an and Hadiths came into existence." writes scientist Bahria.

Our Prophet Muhammad, peace and blessings of God be upon him, was asked about women, their unclear and complicated issues and their rights. Because their rights were completely violated during the period of ignorance. A woman was worthless, like an object in the hands of a man. In the Holy Qur'an, there is enough word as a solution to this situation. It describes all rulings related to women, their rights and duties. In particular, special attention was paid to the issues related to treating them well and taking care of them. Including

"O Muhammad, they ask you for a fatwa about women. Tell them that Allah and the verses about orphan girls recited in the Qur'an give you a fatwa about them!" (Surah Nisa, verse 127).

"It is not lawful for you to inherit wives compulsorily." (Surah Nisa, verse 19)[3.]

Even today, our women are selfless in raising children in various fields and neighborhoods. In recent years, a number of laws, decrees and decisions have been adopted in order to ease their burden and ensure their rights and interests. A woman and her place in the society, country and life is defined as one of the most important directions in the development strategy. In order to carry out their execution in a systematic manner, in each quarter, the

Presidential Decree "On the establishment of the State Committee for Family and Women" was signed.

The role of women, their political and legal culture is of particular importance in the chain of development of Uzbekistan as a state and society, which has a worthy place among the countries of the world and in the international community. Realizing this acute reality, new conditions and opportunities are being created in our country for women to engage in education and science. In particular, a clear example of this is the creation of the "Society of Women Scientists" in order to encourage women and inspire them to science. It is a fact that 50 billion soums have been allocated from the state budget in order to further encourage and support the activities of this society, which in the hearts of all women will strengthen their desire to become the most active layer of the society - a "scientist woman".

With the Decree "On measures to further accelerate work on the systematic support of family and women" in 2022-2026, on increasing the activity of women in all aspects of the economic, political and social life of the country The national program and the comprehensive action plan aimed at the implementation of the national program in 2022-2023 were approved. Laws "On guarantees of equal rights and opportunities for women and men", "On protection of women from harassment and violence" have been adopted in our country. Also, Uzbekistan joined all international documents that protect women from any discrimination and humiliation. In this regard, the Geneva Convention "On Maternity Protection", New York Conventions "On the Political Rights of Women" and "On the Elimination of All Forms of Discrimination against Women's Rights", "Trafficking in Human Beings Supplementing the United Nations Convention against Transnational Organized Crime" , especially international documents such as the Protocol on Prevention, Suppression and Punishment of Trafficking in Women and Children. [4. 65] An example of such international documents as the Protocol on Prevention, Suppression and Punishment of Trafficking in Women and Children can be cited. [4. 65] An example of such international documents as the Protocol on Prevention, Suppression and

Punishment of Trafficking in Women and Children can be cited. [4. 65]

Since 2020, the "Women's register" system has been launched, and the women included in it are being provided with socio-economic, medical and legal assistance. For the years 2022-2024, the "Business Women" program has been adopted, and 8 trillion soums have been allocated for its implementation, preferential loans have been allocated to women. Today, the share of women in the management sector of our country is 27 percent. We can see this as a clear proof that the concept of gender equality in our country is slowly getting absorbed into the psyche of our people. For this purpose, the "Republican commission on increasing the role of women in society, gender equality and family issues" was established in Uzbekistan. The level of gender equality and protection of women's rights in Uzbekistan is recognized at the world level. [p. 4.34]

How far the society has progressed and changed, it can be seen from the treatment of women in this country. After all, women can preserve the honor of the country, the justice of the state, the sincerity in the society and between people with their strong will, care, enthusiasm and tireless efforts.

References:

1. Ibrahimova O.- "Kuch Adolatda" newspaper, January 7, 2022.
2. Yusupova D., Sirojiddinov Sh., Davlatov O. "Navoiyshunoslik". - Tashkent: "Tamaddun"; -2019.
3. "Holy Qur'an" - Uzbek annotated translation.-T.: Cholpon. 1992., pp. 108-135.
4. Kadirkhanova M., Otakhanov F. "A woman and her role in the life of society has always been an important criterion" -

Eshmurzayeva Barno is the student of the Faculty of Uzbek Language and Literature of JDPU named after A. Qadiri. She is the daughter of Barno Osman.

www.ingramcontent.com/pod-product-compliance
Lightning Source LLC
LaVergne TN
LVHW010418070526
838199LV00064B/5338